CUSTOMIZE YOUR CLOTHES

Emma Warren

EMMA WARREN

Photography by Kim Lightbody

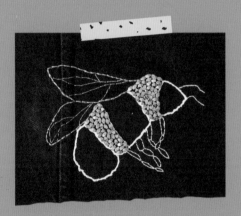

KYLE BOOKS

CUSTOMIZE YOUR CLOTHES

20 hand embroidery projects to update your wardrobe

An Hachette UK Company
www.hachette.co.uk

First published in Great Britain in 2019
by Kyle Books, an imprint of Kyle Cathie Ltd
Carmelite House,
50 Victoria Embankment,
London, EC4Y 0DZ

www.kylebooks.co.uk

ISBN: 978 0 85783 686 1

Distributed in the US by
Hachette Book Group,
1290 Avenue of the Americas,
4th and 5th Floors,
New York, NY 10104

Distributed in Canada by Canadian Manda
Group, 664 Annette St., Toronto, Ontario,
Canada M6S 2C8

Publisher: Joanna Copestick
Editor: Isabel Gonzalez-Prendergast
Copy Editor: Helena Caldon
Designer: Evi-O.Studio / Susan Le
Photographer: Kim Lightbody
Production: Emily Noto

A Cataloguing in Publication record
for this title is available from
the British Library.

Printed and bound in China

10 9 8 7 6 5 4 3 2 1

Contents

Introduction

There is something really quite special about embroidery. One of the oldest crafts, it has endless possibilities and has rightly earned its seat in the forefront of fashion. Adding even the smallest element to a garment, with some detailing, can instantly transform a simple outfit.

This book provides the perfect introduction to basic hand embroidery techniques in the form of twenty projects that can be extended or simplified to fit whichever garment or accessory you wish. Also featured in this book is a dictionary of freehand embroidery stitches. I'm sure once you have acquired the knowledge of these basic stitches and techniques there will be no stopping you! The lovely thing about embroidery is that with just a few stitches and a little time you can create something really beautiful.

I hope that this book will inspire you to create a wardrobe that reflects you. Anyone can put their hand to embroidery, whether they view themselves as creative or not. Just follow the simple steps in this book, enjoy being guided by the images and have fun updating your wardrobe. Remember that each of these projects will lend itself well to any garment or fabric you want to update, so experiment and have fun!

• **TIPS** 1. Don't be afraid to mess up.
2. These projects are only starting points - think beyond the basics and add touches that will make your pieces reflect you.
3. You don't need to buy new garments for these projects - revamp some of your old clothing.
4. If you do mess up - try, try and try again.

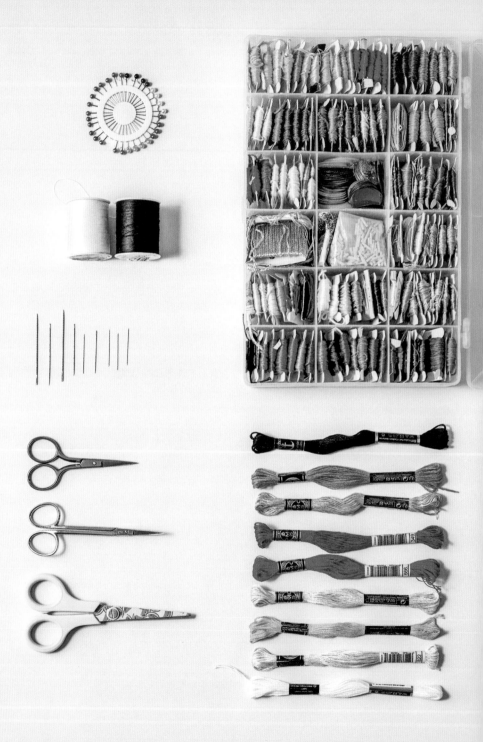

TOOL KIT

I have put together a list of the basic equipment required for the projects in this book. No doubt as you progress your kit will expand. I find myself picking up threads, beads and sequins from charity shops and car boot sales to use for the unique pieces I'm going to create.

NEEDLES

Needles come in a variety of thicknesses and lengths; it is a good idea to have a small selection so you can switch them when needed for different projects and stitches.

TIP If you notice the needle is leaving holes in the fabric, opt for a finer one. If you are having trouble pulling the thread through the fabric, opt for a larger needle. Have a practice on an old piece of clothing or odd piece of fabric to find what works for you.

Embroidery needles – These are of a medium length with a long eye and sharp point. The higher the number on the needle, the finer it is. Medium-length embroidery needles can be used for most general embroidery.

Chenille needles – Used for thicker yarns, ribbons and threads. They are longer in length with a large eye and a sharp point.

Beading needles – Long and fine with a narrow eye for beadwork.

Sharps needles – For hand sewing, these are medium length with a small eye and a sharp point.

THREADS

There are many different types of thread available for embroidery; they come in a variety of thicknesses and materials. You can pick them up in all haberdashery shops or online. I have even spotted a small selection at the local supermarket. Each has its own characteristics and produces different effects, so do experiment!

Cotton embroidery thread – This is the most common embroidery thread; it comes in a wide variety of colours and consists of six strands that can be divided as required. The more strands, the thicker the embroidery, so use fewer strands for fine, delicate embroidery.

Cotton thread – A basic thread that is good to have in your tool kit for tacking when experimenting with appliqué. It is also good to use when adding beads.

Pearl cotton – Made of twisted strands that cannot be divided, this comes in many sizes and has a glossy finish.

Metallic thread – This is used to add a glittery, shiny effect and enhance embroidery. It can be difficult to use as it is more delicate, so it is best to work with shorter lengths to avoid breaks.

SCISSORS

Every project requires scissors.

Fabric scissors – Used for cutting fabric and appliqué.

Small embroidery scissors – Ideal for snipping loose threads and ends.

All-purpose scissors – It's always good to have a normal pair of scissors for cutting tracing paper/carbon paper, which are used to transfer designs from paper to fabric before embroidery (see page 12).

EMBROIDERY HOOPS

Embroidery hoops are used to keep the fabric taut, to allow for even stitching and to reduce puckering and distortion of the fabric. Hoops come in a variety of sizes; whenever possible, choose one that holds the entire design so the hoop does not need to be adjusted before the embroidery is finished. When you are working with repeated designs over a larger area, use smaller hoops that fit the motif you are working on, then move the hoop to work on the next one.

EMBELLISHMENTS

Beads – There are lots of different types of beads to choose from: Bugle beads are tubes that can be smooth or twisted and come in a variety of lengths; Seed beads are round and come in a variety of sizes.

Sequins – Decorative discs with a hole for stitching through, usually in the middle.

Lace/oddments of fabric – I like to keep a box of fabric and lace oddments for appliqué, a technique that involves attaching or adding a layer of fabric or embellishment. It's lovely to mix embroidery with other techniques.

MARKING TOOLS

Water-soluble pens – I almost always use water-soluble pens to transfer my designs onto light fabrics. They contain ink that disappears with water so that any marks that aren't fully covered with stitches can be removed by running the fabric under cold water.

Chalk – Regular chalk or chalk pens are handy for marking on dark fabrics. Any uncovered marks can easily be brushed away when you have finished.

OTHER USEFUL TOOLS

Iron or steamer – To press the finished embroidery.

Dressmaker's pins – To hold the designs in place.

Backing/stabilizer – Stabilizer fabrics are used underneath fabric to add weight and structure. Backing is usually added to the back of the fabric or garment. There are several types available in different weights but there are also different ways of attaching to the fabric – you can use iron-on interfacing or a layer that you can cut or tear away. All add stability to the thinner fabrics, making embroidery easier and helping to avoid puckering.

Tracing paper – Useful for transferring designs.

Tape – For keeping designs in place whilst transferring onto fabric.

Sewing machine and thread – To cut and customize garment shapes.

Carbon paper – Dressmaker's carbon paper is made specifically to transfer designs from paper to fabric.

Old/blank garments – Anything you wish to customize.

HOW TO TRANSFER DESIGNS ONTO FABRIC

You might like to draw directly onto your garment or fabric, however I like to draw onto paper first – that way I can scan the image into my laptop and play around with scale before I transfer it to the fabric. It's a good idea to have a shape to follow as it makes embroidering a lot simpler and less daunting than working on a blank garment.

PREPARING FABRIC

Before embroidering make sure your garment or fabric is crease-free. This will make embroidering easier and ensure a neat finished look.

TRANSFERRING DESIGNS

There are several ways to transfer a design onto fabric; make sure the outline can be covered by your stitches or easily removed once you are finished.

1. Using dressmaker's carbon paper – This is my preferred way as it is super simple. The paper comes in a variety of colours; choose white to transfer onto dark fabrics and a darker colour for light fabrics. Place the fabric on a flat surface, right side up. Place a sheet of carbon paper face down onto the fabric and your design on top of the carbon paper, facing up. Carefully go over your design with a pencil or a pen without ink – press firmly and repeat if areas do not transfer. Use tape or dressmaker's pins to tack the design at the top.

2. Using a light box – You can directly trace your design onto your fabric or garment using a light box, or if you don't have one, use a window!

3. Using a water-soluble pen – You can draw directly onto a garment using the water-soluble pen, or with light garments place the design underneath and trace over it using the pen. Once you have finished the embroidery, wash away any visible pen.

4. Using tracing paper – Outline your design on the tracing paper, place onto fabric and pin to prevent the design moving. Embroider on top of the paper and gently pull away the paper once you have finished.

DESIGN DECISIONS

You might choose to follow these projects exactly as they are but if you have your own designs there are a few things to consider before customizing your garments.

1. Resizing the design – You could use a photocopier to enlarge or reduce the design. Scanning it into your computer and resizing it is another option.

2. Placement – Consider where the design might look best. I like to print my design onto paper so I can pin it to areas of the garment to see where it should go before I start embroidering.

WORKING WITH THREADS

The projects within this book use two types of thread: cotton embroidery and metallic. You can use any thread for any project – try both to see what you like.

DIVIDING EMBROIDERY THREADS

For thicker embroidery use the full six strands; for finer embroidery you will want to divide the thread into finer strands. I like to mix up the thickness of threads used within a design to add a contrast in stitches, which can help to add shading or a 3D element to the design.

If you plan to divide your thread, begin by cutting a length to roughly 40 centimetres (16 inches) – long threads can get worn while stitching and lead to unwanted knots. Hold one end of the thread in one hand and separate the strands with the other. Pull the threads one by one, combining them to achieve the desired thickness.

BEGINNING AND ENDING DESIGNS

I start and end my embroidery with a simple knot to the back of the fabric. To begin, thread your needle and tie a knot at the other end. Bring the needle up from the back of the fabric where you would like to start stitching, pull the thread the whole way up so the knot is now touching the back of the fabric. To end a thread, push the needle down through the fabric and knot, then cut away the remaining thread.

BASIC FREEHAND EMBROIDERY STITCHES

This section will give you an overview of some basic embroidery stitches that are used for the projects within this book. There are plenty more stitches that can be used for embroidery, however, these basic stitches – when used in combination or even just using one of them – can create some beautiful and intricate embroidery.

BACK STITCH

This is the basic stitch for outlining embroidery and sewing. It produces a continuous line of stitching and is perfect for many of the projects in this book.

Bring the needle up through the stitch line, insert a short step back and bring it out again at an equal distance in front of the starting point. Repeat.

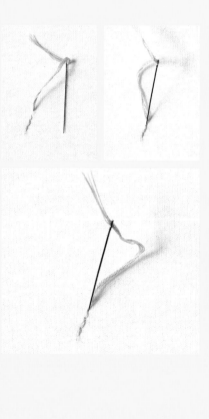

TIPS Although this is quite an easy stitch to learn, it takes practice to make the stitches even. One way to do this is to mark out where the stitches should begin and end using a ruler and water-soluble pen.

Back stitch can also be stitched in rows as a filler stitch; this can be useful when you would like certain areas of your embroidery to stand out more than others. You can also create a thicker outline by stitching two rows of back stitch next to each other.

Experiment with using more or fewer strands of embroidery thread to create finer or bolder embroidery.

STRAIGHT STITCH

This stitch is as simple as bringing the needle up through the fabric and then going back down further along. It can be used to form shapes like stars or add texture to areas, and it's also a great stitch for simple embroidered slogan designs.

RUNNING STITCH

Running stitch is a simple embroidery stitch that is good for making dashed outlines and adding details to the embroidery – it's also perfect for quick lettering or simple motifs.

For running stitch, bring your needle through from the back side of the fabric to the front at your starting point. Go back down a short distance from the first point to complete a single stitch. Continue, making the stitches an equal length and evenly spaced. For a quicker method you can just weave the needle in and out of the fabric, loading several evenly spaced stitches onto the needle at once.

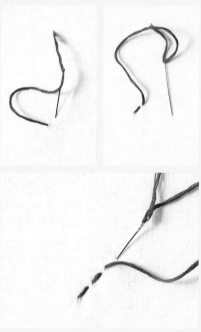

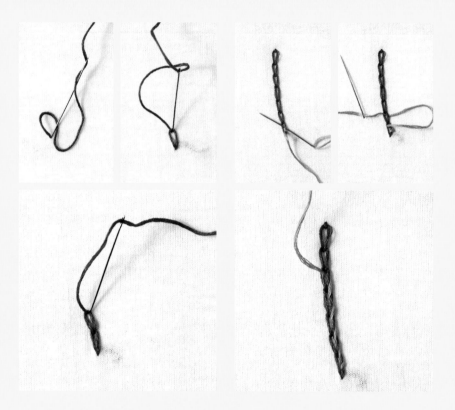

CHAIN STITCH

This is a looped stitch; for a basic chain stitch, bring the needle up through the fabric at your starting point, then take the needle back through to the same point. Bring the tip up through the fabric a short distance away. Place the working thread behind the needle and pull the needle through the loop. Repeat the process to make additional stitches and end the length by making a small anchoring straight stitch at the end of the final loop to secure it in place.

WHIPPED CHAIN STITCH

Whipped chain stitch is just a variety of chain stitch in which you are adding another thread that can be in a contrasting colour or texture. Start by embroidering a basic chain stitch, then bring your thread out of the base of the chain stitch and 'whip' the stitch by passing the thread under each chain stitch from whichever direction you feel most comfortable. Do this without picking up any fabric, just run the needle right under each individual stitch, always passing the needle under the chain stitches from the same direction. You can double whip your chain stitch by first working around the outside of your chain stitches and then working around the central stitches – this way you could use two different colours.

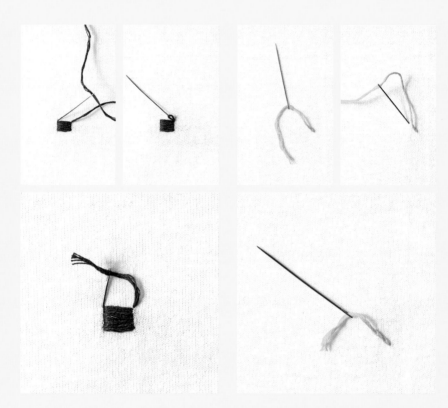

SATIN STITCH

A stitch used to fill areas. For basic satin stitch, bring the needle up through the fabric at your starting point, insert the needle again across from the original entry point, on the opposite side of the shape you are filling. Bring the needle up on the side of the shape where you started and go back down on the opposite side. Repeat the process to make additional stitches.

SPLIT STITCH

This is a neat little stitch that's perfect for lettering or making edges neat. I used this stitch for the star cap outline on page 50 to make the star more defined. It looks more complicated than it is; simply bring the needle up from the back of the fabric and down just as you would in straight stitch, but then bring the needle back up in the centre of the stitch you have just created, splitting the thread. Repeat.

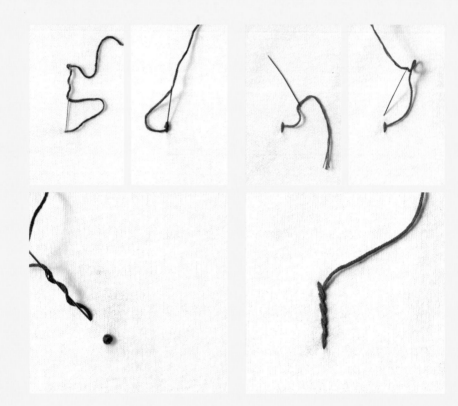

FRENCH KNOT

French knot is a lovely decorative stitch; I use it in the dog t-shirt on page 46 for the eyes but it's also useful to build up texture by placing multiple knots together.

For this stitch, bring the threaded needle up underneath the fabric, holding the thread taut, then wind the thread a couple of times quite tightly around the needle tip. Still holding the wrapped thread, insert the needle back down so that the twists lie neatly on top of the fabric. Repeat as required.

TIP For a smaller knot, wrap the thread only once; for a larger knot you can wrap a few more times.

STEM STITCH

Stem stitch is lovely to use in floral designs. Bring the needle up from behind the fabric and down to regular stitch length as required, then bring the needle back up halfway between stitch one and two –but don't split the thread like split stitch, just place it next to the stitch line – then repeat. Each stitch should be the same length and should begin halfway along the previous stitch.

TIP Do not pull the stitches too tight or it will pull the fabric and cause some puckering. You could add a layer of backing to avoid this and provide some stability.

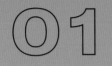

LETTERING

01

SLOGAN
T-SHIRT

Slogan t-shirts have been popular for a while now, whether they are bold and printed or subtly embroidered. Of course, I prefer an embroidered slogan t-shirt! It's a great simple way to revamp an old or basic t-shirt and make a plain outfit a little more interesting.

The best thing about this project is you can embroider just about any design, in any colour or font, making it unique to you. Slogan t-shirts look great styled with some high-waisted jeans.

HOW TO

materials
— Pencil and paper
— T-shirt
— Chalk
— Dressmaker's carbon paper
— Backing/stabilizing fabric
— Embroidery hoop
— Embroidery needle
— 1 embroidery thread (red)

stitches
— Back stitch (4 strands)

1. Write out the slogan you would like to embroider, or use the French slogan I have used: 'la vie est belle', which translates as: 'life is beautiful'.

2. Choose the placement on the t-shirt; I have opted for mid-chest, roughly 10 centimetres (4 inches) down from the neckline. You can mark this with a little chalk dot.

3. Transfer your design using dressmaker's carbon paper. Add a small amount of backing and fix the embroidery hoop in place.

4. Thread the embroidery needle with the desired amount of strands – I used four.

5. Using back stitch, follow the lines from the transferred carbon paper – try to cover the lines so they cannot be seen once complete.

6. Remove the embroidery hoop and steam or press the fabric to remove the hoop mark and any creasing.

TIP Use six embroidery strands for a bolder slogan or use fewer for a more subtle stitch line.

02

CONVERSATIONAL
COLLAR

Why not let your collars do the talking? This super simple project is a lovely way to embellish a collar and make a statement or just a silly embroidered 'Hi', without actually having to say a thing. It's a conversation starter as well as a cute collar. I thought this would be a lovely project because many people express themselves through their style, so why not use embroidery to express yourself?

Embellished collars can be expensive to buy on the high street, so dig out your old blouses or shirts and add a little detail.

HOW TO

materials

- Pencil and Dressmaker's carbon paper or water-soluble pen
- Blouse or shirt with a collar
- Backing/stabilizing fabric
- Small embroidery hoop
- Embroidery needle
- 1 embroidery thread (lilac)

stitches

- Running stitch (6 strands)
- French knot (6 strands)

1. Transfer your chosen slogan onto your collared garment using either carbon paper or a water-soluble pen – whichever method you prefer and suits the colour of the garment.

2. Add a small amount of backing and fix in place with a small embroidery hoop on one side of the collar.

3. Thread the needle with six strands of embroidery thread in the colour of your choice – using six strands will make the slogan pop and stand out a little more.

4. Use a simple running stitch to embroider the letters – try to keep the stitches and distance between each stitch the same size.

5. If, like me, you're embroidering 'Hi', add a French knot to dot the 'i'.

6. Repeat on the other collar!

● TIPS   1.   Personalize a collar with
                  your initials!
             2.   Use split stitch for a more
                  3D look to the letters.

03

SLOGAN TOTE BAG

You can never have enough tote bags. I often swap my handbag for a tote, especially on Saturdays to fill with all my market treats. Plain tote bags are affordable and make for the perfect blank base for you to embellish or even have a practice on.

Why not embroider a slogan on one side and a plant on the other? You could also add a pom pom key ring for an extra bit of colour.

HOW TO

1. Transfer your design using a water-soluble pen – the fabric for my bag was thin enough that I could just place the design under the fabric and trace it.
2. Add a layer of backing and a large embroidery hoop that will fit the whole slogan.
3. Thread your needle with the colour thread of your choice, using all six embroidery strands.
4. Stitch each letter of your slogan using split stitch, then add another optional row of split stitch next to the original row to make the text stand out.

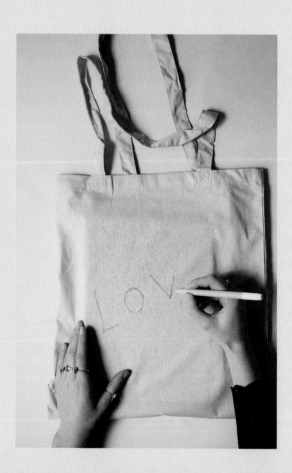

1. You could opt for using running stitch for a super quick slogan on the bag, too.
2. Instead of a slogan, take the sharks from the skirt project on page 84 and embroider those all over a tote!

Additional pom pom key ring

1. To create a pom pom, either follow the pom pom maker instructions (see page 105), or cut a rectangle out of cardboard, then cut a slit halfway down the middle (the bigger the rectangle, the bigger the pom pom).

2. Wrap your wool around the centre of the rectangle – the amount you wrap will determine the thickness of the pom pom. When the wool is wrapped around the cardboard, tie a knot in the centre using the slit and tie around the wrapped wool.

3. Slide the wool off the cardboard rectangle and tie the centre again even tighter. Use scissors to cut the looped ends – it will look a little uneven at this stage – then trim the wool to make an even pom pom!

4. Now taking the pom poms you have made, arrange and tie them onto a key ring. You could add beads or a little charm to finish, if you like. Then, just attach the keyring to your tote.

04

MONO-GRAMMED SWEATER

Monogramming with initials has always been a popular trend. This project would be a lovely way to add that personalized element to a look or it would make a thoughtful gift for a friend. I love the contrast of bold thick stitches mixed with the finer stitches to make the letter really pop.

I have chosen to embroider my initial onto a sweater, but a canvas accessory bag would be the perfect alternative. That is what is lovely about the projects in this book, you can mix and match as these designs work on any garment.

HOW TO

materials		stitches	
— Paper and pencil — Chalk — Dressmaker's carbon paper — Sweater — Backing/stabilizing fabric — Embroidery hoop — Embroidery needle — 1 embroidery thread (red)		— Split stitch (4 strands) — Chain stitch (4 strands) — Back stitch (2 strands) — Satin stitch (4 strands)	

1. Draw out your letter/design onto paper, decide where you would like the placement on the sweater and mark with a chalk dot, if needed.
2. Transfer your design using dressmaker's carbon paper.
3. Add a piece of backing behind the fabric and an embroidery hoop that fits the entire design.
4. Thread the embroidery needle with four strands of thread for split stitch, which I used for the whole of the 'E'.
5. I then added a second row of split stitch so the letter would stand out from the florals, but this is optional.
6. Build up a floral pattern in chain stitch – which is often called lazy daisy stitch (perfect for florals!).
7. Keep a copy of the design nearby for reference but you may wish to add more or fewer chain stitches to make up petals and leaves as you go.
8. For the finer florals use two strands of embroidery thread and back stitch the petals.

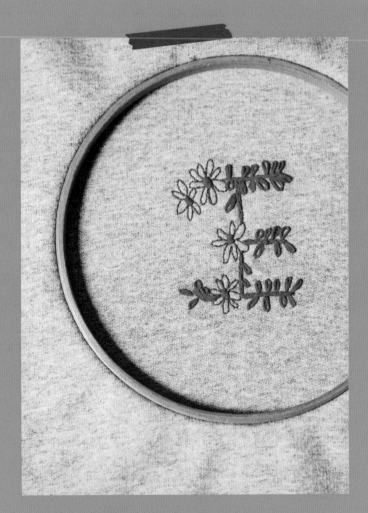

9. Use satin stitch to fill the centres of the flowers to make them pop!
10. Finish on the back of the hoop with a knot and remove the hoop.

11. Steam or press the design to finish to remove hoop marks or creases.

05

CIAO JACKET

I love to add detail to the back of jackets and this one is no exception. This emerald-green jacket is one I have had in my wardrobe for a while – it still had the tag on and for some reason I just haven't reached for it. I love the colour and the bomber-jacket shape is timeless, so I thought why not add a slogan to the back to jazz it up a little? You could embroider any slogan or motif you like; these types of embellished jackets can cost a fortune to buy on the high street, but with a little time and embroidery you could recreate one yourself for only the cost of some thread. You can often pick up vintage-style bombers in charity shops, too.

Also, adding detail to the back makes for the perfect excuse for a twirl picture!

HOW TO

materials		stitches	

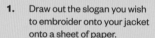	— Paper and pencil
	— Dressmaker's carbon paper
	— Jacket
	— Backing/stabilizing fabric
	— Embroidery hoop
	— Embroidery needle
	— 1 embroidery thread (cream)
	— 1 metallic embroidery thread
	   or contrasting colour
			— Split stitch (6 strands)
			— Chain stitch (6 strands)
			— Double whipped chain
			   stitch (gold)

1. Draw out the slogan you wish to embroider onto your jacket onto a sheet of paper.
2. Transfer the design onto the jacket – this is when it is useful to have your slogan on paper, so you can move it around on the jacket to figure out the perfect placement. Use white carbon dressmaker's paper to transfer the design onto dark fabric – this works really well with satin so you have clear lines to follow.
3. Add a layer of backing and an embroidery hoop, making sure the fabric is as flat as possible.
4. Use spilt stitch to embroider around the slogan using six strands of embroidery thread. This will make the stitch stand out and look almost 3D on the fabric. (You could fill the split stitch with satin stitch if you prefer bolder lettering but I like just having the outline of the letters.)
5. If you would like to add a couple of stars to your jacket back, too, do so by simply transferring them again using the carbon paper technique.
6. Add a little hoop around the first star and work around the shape with chain stitch.

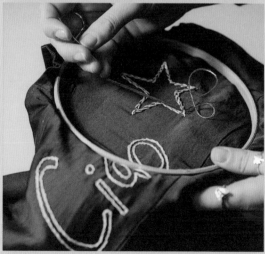

1. When transferring the design onto fabric, add some tape on top of the paper covering the design, as this will stop the paper breaking when adding pressure to the design as you transfer it. It also means the paper can be used again.
2. Add oversized sequins for a more glam-rock, festival look.

7. To add a more decorative element I have added a double whipped chain stitch to the stars using a metallic thread, which adds some glitter to the design, but you can use any thread you like! A contrasting colour or a thicker, more-textured yarn could look lovely.

8. Repeat the steps for as many stars as you would like to add.

9. Remove the hoop and carefully cut away any backing.

MOTIFS

DOG T-SHIRT

Who doesn't love dogs?! This design proudly features my family dog Sophie in the middle. I designed a similar t-shirt to help raise money for a local dog charity and it proved really popular, so I thought it would be a lovely project to include in this book.

You could embroider five dogs, one dog or even a hundred and one Dalmatians! It would make a lovely gift to embroider a friend's pet, too. Feel free to play around with placement – one little dog on the left chest or sleeve could be cute.

This project features my signature embroidery style, which is to use fine, one-colour stitched lines. I love how simple yet detailed the design looks on a basic t-shirt.

HOW TO

materials
— Pencil
— Dressmaker's carbon paper
— T-shirt
— Backing/stabilizing fabric
— Embroidery hoop
— Embroidery needle
— 1 embroidery thread (black)

stitches
— Back stitch (3 strands)
— French knot (3 strands)
— Straight stitch (1 strand)

1. Transfer the design from page 111 onto your garment of choice. I used carbon paper as I find it the easiest transfer method on darker-coloured garments.
2. Add a layer of backing behind the fabric, then fix on the embroidery hoop.
3. Thread the needle with three strands of embroidery thread – this creates a finer stitch line for the dog outlines. Work around the design using back stitch, trying to keep the stitches to a similar length so that the design looks neat.
4. Stitch French knots for the eyes, wrapping the thread around twice to create the knot (see page 20).

● **TIPS**   1.   Feel free to use satin stitches or thicker
                   outlines - you could build up lots of French
                   knots to create a fur-like texture!
             2.   Make stitches smaller at the edges for a curved
                   appearance and fewer sharp corners.

5. For the Dalmatian spots use a combination of French knot with straight stitch on top to flatten the knot a little so they are not as pronounced as the eyes.

6. Repeat the stitches on each dog. I find it easier to stitch all the outlines in the back stitch first then work on the finer detailing with the French knots.

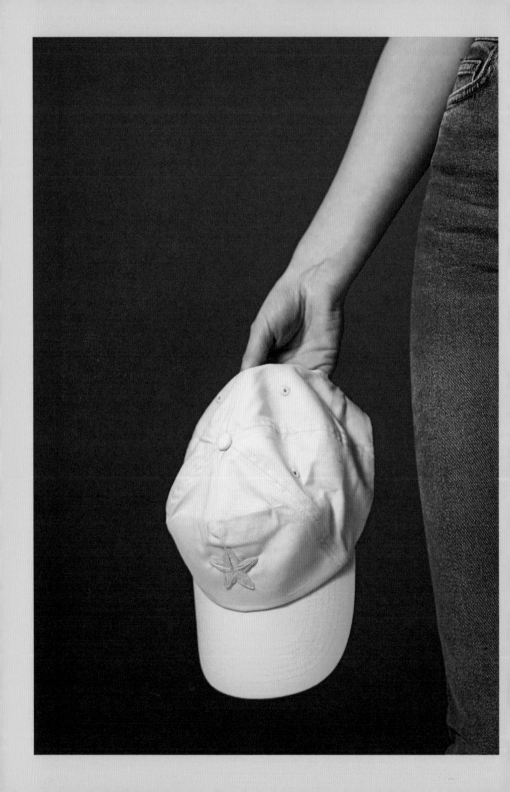

07

STAR
CAP

Embroidery has always had a place in my heart, but it seems to be firmly in the spotlight at the moment – it can be seen not only all over the catwalks but on the high street, too. You can add embroidery to just about anything to update an item or to give it a twist. This project takes a cap and adds a simple star motif using three basic stitches.

HOW TO

materials

- Pencil, paper and Dressmaker's carbon paper or water-soluble pen
- Cap/hat
- Ruler
- Embroidery needle
- 1 embroidery thread (yellow)

stitches

- Straight stitch (6 strands)
- Satin stitch (6 strands)
- Split stitch (6 strands

1. Draw out and transfer the design onto the cap. This is a little trickier than on other embroidery projects as a cap isn't flat! I drew a star onto paper, pinned it onto the cap and stitched through the paper, but you could use a water-soluble pen and draw directly onto the fabric if you prefer.

2. Split the star into five sections with a ruler to make the embroidered satin stitch sections a little easier.

3. Stitch the outline of the star using a long straight stitch; you can then remove the paper.

4. Next, begin filling each section of the star using satin stitch. Working around the star in sections makes the satin stitch look a lot neater.

5. Finally, work around the star with split stitch – this creates a braided, slightly raised outline and tidies up the overall design. That's it!

● **TIPS**   1. You could just work the
            star as an outline using
            split stitch.
         2. Florals would also look
            super cute on a cap.

08

DAISY CHAIN SLEEVES

We all have too many plain t-shirts in our wardrobe. This project takes an old t-shirt and gives it a new lease of life with a simple daisy chain design that wraps around each sleeve. Alternatively, you could simply add trims or lace trim to sleeves for a super quick, instant update, as adding lace to a garment can give a more luxurious look to a basic t-shirt. I drew out this sweet daisy chain design, which could be added to the hem of the entire t-shirt or just used on elements as I have done with the sleeves. This design reminds me of a holiday friendship bracelet.

HOW TO

<table>
<tr><td>materials</td><td>
— Dressmaker's carbon paper
— T-shirt
— Backing/stabilizing fabric
— Small embroidery hoop
— Embroidery needle
— 2 embroidery threads
  (white, yellow)
</td><td>stitches</td><td>
— Stem stitch (6 strands)
— Split stitch (6 strands)
— Back stitch (2 strands)
</td></tr>
</table>

1. If you are embroidering on a black t-shirt as I have here, use white dressmaker's carbon paper to transfer your design to the edge of the sleeves. Add the backing and use a small hoop to work on areas of the design at a time – as the design is on the sleeve this can make manoeuvring around the design slightly trickier because there isn't as much space to stitch as there would be to a t-shirt hem. Using a smaller hoop maximizes the space left for your stitches.

2. Use six strands of white embroidery thread and stitch the stem of the daisy chain using stem stitch to create a twisted stitch kind of look.

3. Use six strands of yellow embroidery thread and outline the flower centres using split stitch. This stitch creates a raised surface, making the yellow centres pop from the black t-shirt.

4. For the flower petals, use two strands of white embroidery thread and work around the outline using small back stitches to create a delicate flower which will contrast with the bolder stem and split stitch.

5. Remove the hoop and move it around the t-shirt, repeating the steps above to complete the design.

6. Repeat on the other sleeve.

● **TIP** Add the daisy chain to a neckline or the entire length of the t-shirt hem.

09

PALM TREE ACCESSORY BAG

Little zippered bags or pouches are perfect for keeping makeup, stationery and any random bits and bobs in that you want to tidy away – or maybe your newly acquired embroidery kit! They also make lovely gifts.

Here I've opted for a simple palm tree design that I have repeated in a group of three to create a pattern, using red, orange and yellow to add to the summery feel. Again, you can embroider just about anything onto a bag, so have fun and experiment. This is a project that requires minimal materials as the canvas-like fabric is the perfect surface for embroidery – you don't need a hoop or backing fabric. This could be a good project to start with to practise your techniques!

HOW TO

materials
— Pencil
— Dressmaker's carbon paper
— Plain canvas pouch
— Embroidery needle
— 3 embroidery threads
   (yellow, red, orange)

stitches
— Back stitch (6 strands)
— Straight stitch
   (6 strands)

1. Transfer the design on page 110 using dressmaker's carbon paper. I find this technique works really well and leaves you the perfect line to follow, but you can use another method if you prefer.

2. Thread the needle using six strands of embroidery thread. Using back stitch, work around the shape in whichever colour you prefer. Work straight stitch across the tree trunk.

3. Repeat on the other two palms to create a pattern. You could use the same colour thread for all, but I have used a different one for each palm tree.

4. Fill your pouch with bits and bobs!

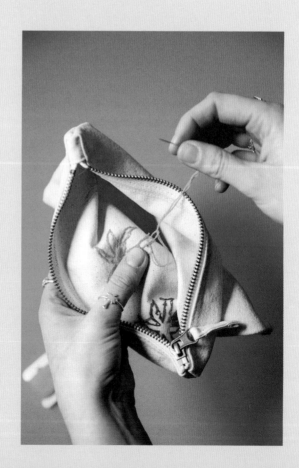

● **TIPS** 1. Using smaller stitches allows
             you to work around curves and edges
             without making them appear sharp.
          2. You could add some fabric paint
             with your embroidery or use a satin
             stitch for a bold pop of colour
             and texture.

Palm Tree Accessory Bag — 61

10

ROSE SLEEVE

It's all in the small details. There is no need to spend hours and hours creating an embroidery masterpiece to transform a garment. Adding little elements to clothing can create a subtle detail that makes the piece truly unique. I opted to use metallic thread to add a little extra sparkle to this sleeve. Embroidering on a sleeve can be a little trickier because you don't have lots of free fabric, but the extra effort is worth it for a design that will make your shirt stand out from the crowd.

HOW TO

materials
— Pencil and paper
— Dressmaker's carbon paper
— Sweater
— Small embroidery hoop
— Backing/stabilizing fabric
— Embroidery needle
— 1 metallic embroidery   thread (gold)

stitches
— Stem stitch
— Chain stitch
— Back stitch

1. Once you have decided on the placement, transfer the design on page 110 using dressmaker's carbon paper. I used white carbon paper to transfer onto a black garment as it could be easily seen.
2. Add some backing and place the prepared fabric into a small embroidery hoop just big enough for the design so that you have maximum space in the sleeve to work. I used a 10 centimetre (4 inch) hoop.
3. Thread the needle with metallic thread – this can be a little tricky (see tips).
4. Use stem stitch for the stem of the rose and chain stitch for leaves.
5. Back stitch the petals, trying to keep the stitches equal for a more polished look.
6. Remove the hoop and steam or press the design to finish to remove hoop marks or creases.

1. To help thread the metallic thread onto the needle, add a little bit of tape to the end first, as this will keep the strands together. Remember to cut away the tape before you start embroidering.
2. Add a rose on each sleeve or embroider a design all around the cuff.

WILDLIFE

11

PLANT
T-SHIRT

I love plants! I have/did have lots in my home, but I find them impossible to keep alive! You can count on this cute customized t-shirt, knowing it will definitely not die on you. This design is actually one of the most popular that I sell. This project uses only one type of stitch to create a simple addition to a basic t-shirt. I love seeing what a simple stitch can bring to such an easy line drawing.

HOW TO

1. Using a water-soluble pen or pencil and paper, transfer the design on page 110 onto the chosen t-shirt. I used a white t-shirt, which made it easy to trace my drawn paper image through the fabric using the pen.

2. Add a layer of backing behind the fabric, then fix on the embroidery hoop.

3. Thread the needle with a green embroidery thread using all six strands and follow the drawn lines with back stitch.

4. Once the design is complete, remove the hoop and run the fabric under water to remove any visible pen. The beauty of a water-soluble pen is that it completely disappears with water, so if you decide to stray a little from your original design when you start stitching you can do so without leaving any trace.

● **TIP** Try to keep the stitches to a similar size so the design stays really neat.

12

FLORAL TRAINERS

A pair of white trainers is something the majority of us have in our wardrobe, or you can pick up a pair super cheap! This project updates an affordable pair of trainers, making them look more expensive and even designer-esque with only a few simple stitches. I opted for a repeated pattern of a flower all over, randomly placed. You could also use motifs from previous projects or create your own. How lovely would fine-line, black-stitched bugs look all over a white trainer for a monochrome look?

This project uses minimal materials, there is no need for a hoop or backing material as the canvas fabric makes for the perfect embroidery backing. Manoeuvring around the shoe can be tricky, so opt for a simple design for your first try. I am sure once you have had a bit of practice the possibilities will be endless and you will never own a blank trainer again!

HOW TO

materials		stitches	

— Trainers
— Water-soluble pen
  (not essential)
— Embroidery needle
— 4 embroidery threads
  (yellow, blue, mint green,
  dark blue)
		— French knot (6 strands)
		— Chain stitch
		  (4 or 6 strands)	

1. Dig out an old pair of trainers; I put mine in the washing machine, which seemed to give them a new lease of life!
2. You could mark out little dots using a water-soluble pen to work out where you would like your daisies, but I just went for a random pattern without marking beforehand.
3. Thread an embroidery needle with a colour of your choice for the centres of the flowers; I used the full six strands as I wanted the centres to stand out.
4. Start stitching French knots randomly all over the shoe – as many or as few as you wish – to make the flower centres.

TIPS

1. You could stick to having the design down one side of the shoe or just on the tongue rather than all over for a more subtle look.
2. As a super simple DIY project you could stitch lots of multi-coloured French knots all over for a spotty trainer!
3. Use up odd lengths of thread from previous projects when stitching French knots as they use very little thread.

5. Next, work on the petals for each flower, repeating chain stitches in a colour of your choice to build up the petals, also known as lazy daisy stitch. You could go multi-coloured or stick to one shade. Use four strands for a finer petal shape or six for a bolder flower. You could mix up the stitches using different thicknesses and sizes.

6. Tidy up any loose threads and, voila, brand new trainers!

13

FLORAL POCKET

This little customization uses several basic stitches in combination to update a plain pocket t-shirt. Whether you embroider a single rose or a whole bunch bursting out of the pocket like I have here, it will add a cute colour injection to your otherwise plain garment. Feel free to experiment by adding more colour and florals – you could even embroider a cute animal peeking out of the pocket.

HOW TO

materials		stitches	
— Water-soluble pen — Plain t-shirt with a pocket — Backing/stabilizing fabric — Embroidery hoop — Embroidery needle — 6 embroidery threads 　(green, blue, pale green, 　yellow, red, orange)		— Stem stitch (6 strands) — French knot — Chain stitch (6 strands) — Straight stitch 　(4 strands) — Running stitch 　(4 strands) — Back stitch (4 strands)	

1. Transfer the design from page 110 onto the fabric; for this project I put the paper with the design under the fabric and traced it with a water-soluble pen (I used a white t-shirt because it was easier to trace the design through the fabric), but you can use any of the other methods (see page 12).

2. Add backing fabric if necessary, then add a hoop around the pocket to keep the fabric in one place while embroidering.

3. To stitch the flower stems I used the aptly named stem stitch!

4. To stitch the centres of the flowers or add a little dot of detailing, use French knots – these can be built up to fill a space or spaced out to add intricate detail.

5. I used chain stitch for the petals and leaves as this is perfect for creating curved petal-like shapes.

6. Use a mix of straight stitch, running stitch and back stitch to embroider the floral outlines. It is nice to mix up the stitches you use to add more detail and a textured finish. I personally prefer simpler outlines, but we all have different styles and if you prefer a bolder look you can use satin stitch to fill the shapes.

7. Remove the hoop and cut away any backing.

● **TIP** Use fewer strands of embroidery thread for a more delicate effect or more for a bold design. It is nice to mix up the thickness of strands within the design, as it makes it look more intricate and detailed.

14

WILDFLOWER SWEATER

I bet if you look in your wardrobe you have at least two plain sweaters that you never wear. Adding florals to an old sweater will give it a new lease of life! Florals have always been a popular addition within embroidery and print and I think this design adds a subtle nod to old-style embroidery while updating it with the use of colour and placement. I have used pink embroidery thread here to contrast with the pale blue sweater, which I think gives a floral design a contemporary look.

HOW TO

materials

- Paper and pencil
- Sweater
- Backing/stabilizing fabric
- Embroidery hoop
- Embroidery needle
- 2 embroidery threads (dark pink, pale pink)

stitches

- Back stitch (3 strands)
- Chain stitch (3 strands)
- French knot (6 strands)

1. First, draw out and transfer your design onto a sweater. I opted to draw out my design onto paper and then pin it to the garment and embroider through the paper, removing it later, but you can use any transfer method you prefer (see page 12).

2. Add a layer of backing behind the fabric and fix in place with an embroidery hoop, so you don't have to move it until you have finished.

3. For the stems I used back stitch, using only three strands of embroidery thread to create simple lines.

4. Next, build up lots of chain stitches for the petals – you can go a little off design at this point, feel free to add more or fewer petals to make up the design.

5. Add some French knots for some texture. I used a pale pink thread for these and twisted the thread around three times to create more of a raised knot.

TIP It would be lovely to create an ombre effect using different tones of the same colour.

15

SHARK SKIRT

Repeating a design all over to create the look of a pattern is a lovely way to update an old skirt. I have chosen sharks but you could embroider florals, shapes or anything really!

Who else will have an embroidered shark skirt?

This project uses three basic stitches to create something a little different.

HOW TO

See page 111

materials		stitches	
	— Pencil — Dressmaker's carbon paper — Pins — Skirt — Backing/stabilizing fabric — Embroidery hoop — Embroidery needle — 4 embroidery threads (dark blue, navy, mint green, grey)		— Split stitch (6 strands) — Back stitch (2 strands) — French knot (6 strands)

1. Transfer the design on page 111 using dressmaker's carbon paper and arrange over the garment. It is a good idea to position the paper design and pin it so you can plan out the placement. I went for random placement but you might like to evenly space the sharks all over.

2. Add a layer of backing and position an embroidery hoop so that you can work on one shark at a time.

3. Use split stitch for the outline, threading the needle with all six strands of embroidery thread.

4. Use back stitch for the finer details, for example the gills, dividing out the thread into finer strands. Use two strands of embroidery thread to stitch finer details to contrast the texture of the embroidery with the thicker split stitch outlines.

5. Use French knot for eyes! Wrap the thread two or three times to create the knot.

1. You could use lots of different stitches for each shark to add more interest and detailing.
2. Try to keep the stitches a similar and equal distance and size to keep the embroidery looking neat.
3. The bugs from the bug shirt project on page 98 would look amazing all over a skirt or dress, too.

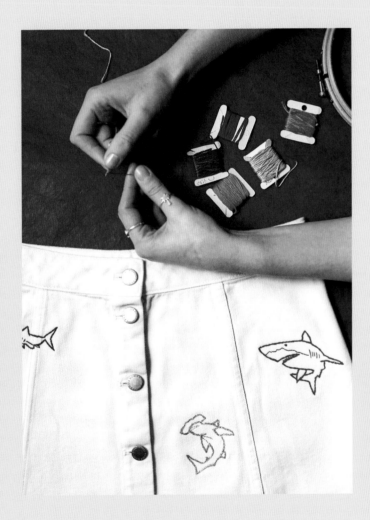

6. Repeat for the other sharks, I used different tones of blue for each shark but this is optional.

Repeat on the back of the skirt if you would like the design all over.

04

EMBELLISHMENT

16

LEMON T-SHIRT

A fruity little project to add some fun to a plain t-shirt. I opted for a lemon design, adding some little beads for detailing and using thick and thin stitch lines to create more of a contrasting 3D look.

For some reason lemons just make me think of being on holiday! They are such a summery fruit. You could embroider any fruit – a pineapple or watermelon would look super cute, too.

HOW TO

materials		stitches	

— Pencil
— Dressmaker's carbon paper
— T-shirt
— Backing/stabilizing fabric
— Embroidery hoop
— Embroidery needle
— 2 embroidery threads
  (black, yellow)
— Black seed beads
  and beading needle
— Cotton thread
  (for attaching beads)
		— Split stitch
		  (6 strands)
		— Back stitch
		  (black - 2 strands/
		  yellow - 6 strands)
		— Running stitch (2
		  strands)
		— Straight stitch (6
		  strands)
		— Satin stitch (6 strands)
		— French knot (6 strands)	

1. Transfer the lemon design on page 110 using dressmaker's carbon paper or your preferred transfer method (see page 12).
2. Add a layer of backing behind the fabric and secure with an embroidery hoop.
3. Thread the embroidery needle with six strands of embroidery thread.
4. Use split stitch for the top outline of the lemon and sliced lemon, for a thicker line.
5. Use back stitch to contrast the stitches for the other side of the lemon and leaves.
6. Use running stitch to add detail to the leaves and satin stitch for the stalk.
7. Re-thread your needle with two strands of embroidery thread and sew the lemon segments using long straight stitches.
8. Using a yellow embroidery thread, build up some straight stitches to add some subtle texture to the design.
9. Add a couple of French knots and small black seed beads for detailing.
10. Remove the hoop and steam out any creases.

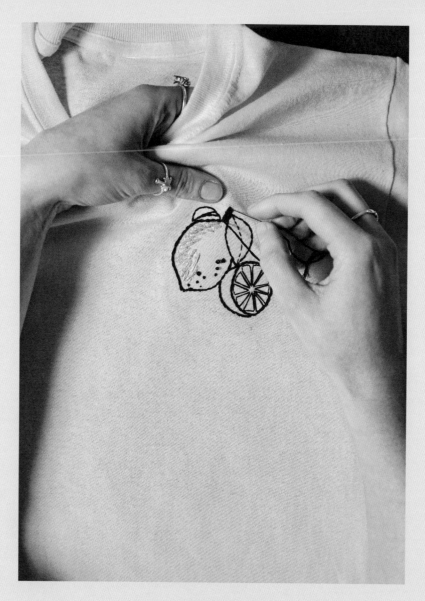

● **TIP** Stitch all thicker stitches
first to avoid having
to re-thread so often.

17

HEART
JEANS

We all have far too many pairs of the same jeans within our wardrobes. I had at least three pairs of pretty much identical high-waist, straight-leg jeans, so I thought this would be the perfect opportunity to add something different to a pair. Again, this is a project you can adapt and experiment with – you could just add some detail to the back pocket or go all out and embroider a pattern all over. I went for adding three hearts to the back of the jeans near the hem. From the front these jeans will look like any other standard pair, but from the back they will look completely unique.

This project uses a technique called cutwork; using denim for this makes it easier as the fabric is sturdy and any fraying will only add to the look. However, you can add a decorative stitch around the cutwork to neaten the edge or add a fray stopper to keep the cut neat. I like the mix of a filled heart, an outline of a heart and then a cut heart, but you could just opt for one simple heart or another shape of your choice.

HOW TO

<table>
<tr><td>materials</td><td>— Pencil and paper
— Dressmaker's carbon paper
— Jeans
— Backing/stabilizing fabric
   (optional)
— Small embroidery hoop
— Embroidery needle
— 1 embroidery thread (red)
— Sharp embroidery scissors</td><td>stitches</td><td>— Split stitch (6 strands)
— Satin stitch (6 strands)
— Back stitch (6 strands)
— Running stitch (6 strands)</td></tr>
</table>

1. Draw out and transfer your design onto the jeans; I used white dressmaker's carbon paper which showed up really well on the blue jean fabric.

2. Add a layer of backing for stability – this is not essential if your jeans are of heavy weight but you might find it makes embroidery a little easier.

3. Add an embroidery hoop. I would normally recommend using a hoop that fits the entire design, but when embroidering on a leg or sleeve there is little room to manoeuvre so it is better to use a small hoop and work on each heart individually. Thread the needle with six strands of red embroidery thread and stitch around the first heart using split stitch. I chose this stitch as it has a raised appearance, making the heart look 3D. It is also a great stitch to use as a base for satin stitch.

4. Fill the heart using satin stitch with the same red thread, stitching over and through the split stitch you have just embroidered. Satin stitch looks a lot more complicated than it is; it's pretty much lots of straight stitches built up next to each other.

1. Add a second row of split stitch to the first heart to add more of a 3D look.
2. You could add a slogan on the bottom of the legs - the possibilities are endless. Experiment!

5. Move the hoop around the second heart and use back stitch for a simple outline. Try to keep the stitches equal in size; this will make the whole heart look a lot neater.
6. Move the embroidery hoop to the final heart and work around the design with a simple running stitch.
7. Using a small pair of sharp embroidery scissors, cut the heart shape out leaving the backing intact a little distance from the running stitch.

8. Work around the heart with satin stitch from the inside of the heart to the outside to avoid fraying. (You could leave with just a running stitch and add some fray stop to the edges.)
9. Remove the hoop and backing.
10. Repeat on the other jean leg.
11. Now you have a unique pair of jeans!

18

BUG
SHIRT

Bugs and beetles have been a massive trend not only in my own work but everywhere else, too, so I just had to include a bug project in this book. I love the idea of adding small amounts of embellishment to create big impact. A white shirt is another fashion staple, so why not add something different? This project combines simple stitches with some beading to create a jewelled look for an old shirt or blouse.

I have chosen this oversized shirt-style dress so it could be worn in a number of ways – tied up for a cropped look or worn loose over jeans.

You can embroider a simple single bug design here or go for a more complex-looking one with lots of bugs. I have used a mix of finer and thicker stitches to encapsulate the detailed and delicate nature of the bugs.

HOW TO

materials	stitches
— Pencil — Dressmaker's carbon paper — Backing/stabilizing fabric — Shirt or shirt dress — Small embroidery hoop — Embroidery needle — 1 embroidery thread (black) — Black seed beads and beading needle — Cotton thread (for attaching beads)	— Back stitch (2 strands) — Satin stitch (6 strands) — Straight stitch (2 strands) — French knot (6 strands)

1. Decide which bugs you would like to embroider from page 111 and where you want to place them.
2. Trace out your bugs on dressmaker's carbon paper and when you're happy with them, transfer them. I used blue pen so that it would show up the detail when embroidering.
3. Add your backing and then hoop up the bug you are embroidering first.
4. For the moth wings on the collar, separate the embroidery thread to stitch the outline with just two strands to give a finer outline using back stitch.
5. Use satin stitch for the main body and for a more defined shape use spilt stitch around the outside of the satin stitch.
6. Add beads by adding one basic stitch, then attaching the bead before knotting underneath to secure. I added a line of beads to contrast with the stitched lines.

◉ **TIP**   Add some metallic thread
            for extra detailing.

7. Use French knots to add details
    to the moth wings; wrap the
    thread once for a small knot
    and three times for a large knot.

8. Add as many or as few bugs
    to your shirt as you wish.

9. Remove your hoop and steam
    garment to finish.

19

POM POM SWEATER

You can add pom poms to just about anything! This is a fun and easy way to transform an old sweater by bringing a playful element to something plain.

You can go mad with this project. Play with scale, colour or even arrange the pom poms to create a shape or slogan. I chose a sweater with balloon sleeves with more of a chunky knit to balance out the mid-sized pom poms I created, which I then randomly stitched all over. I just love how fun this customization is. The pom pom possibilities are endless!

The easiest way to make lots of pom poms is with a pom pom maker – you can pick up a set of these rings very cheaply at any craft or haberdashery shop. I love to sit in front of the TV with some wool and my pom pom maker and just get lost in the craft.

HOW TO

materials

- Pom pom maker (see page 35
  for instructions without
  a pom pom maker)
- Wool yarn in your choice
  of colours - use one
  or a few different shades
- Old sweater
- Pins
- Cotton sewing thread
  and needle

1. Do not wrap the wool too tight!
2. Swap out pom poms for beads and sequins and randomly stitch them all over in the same way. Have fun!

1. Using a pom-pom maker, open the rings and place them on top of each other.
2. Wrap one side of the pom-pom maker with wool – you can use more than one colour if you wish. Go wild! Then wrap the second side of the maker.
3. Close the two halves together, connecting the closure fully.
4. Cut open the pom pom along the outside.
5. Take a length of wool and tie it in a knot around the bundle.
6. Remove the pom pom from the maker and tidy up by trimming any uneven edges.
7. Organize your pom poms however you wish on the sweater. I opted to randomly place them all over the front and back but you could just add them to the sleeves, if you prefer.
8. Position them in place with safety pins or dressmaker's pins, then secure them with a couple of stitches using a needle and thread, or use the piece of wool you used to tie around the pom pom to add a stitch into the sweater if it's of a heavier weight.

20

QUEEN BEE JACKET

I adore bees! In fact, my bestselling t-shirt is a bumble bee design. My house, my jewellery, my wardrobe, are all filled with bee motifs – even my dog is named 'Bea' – and this book just wouldn't be complete without me adding some. So I decided to go big! I embellished two giant bees onto the back of an old black denim jacket I've had in my wardrobe for ages, which

I kind of fell out of love with (that's the beauty of updating and customizing old clothing, you can give it a new lease of life so you love it again). This project allows you to experiment and play with all of the techniques you have learned throughout the book. More is more in this case – I have even added gold beads and gold metallic thread!

HOW TO

materials	stitches
– Pencil and paper – Dressmaker's carbon paper – Jacket – Backing/stabilizing fabric (optional) – Large embroidery hoop – Embroidery needle – 1 embroidery thread (white) – 1 metallic embroidery thread (gold) – Gold beads and beading needle – Cotton thread for attaching beads	– Split stitch (6 strands) – Back stitch (white - 2 strands, metallic gold) – Running stitch (6 strands)

1. Start by mapping out where you would like your bees; I scanned my drawing into my laptop and resized the bees so I could place the paper version on the jacket back and have a better view of how the design could look.

2. Transfer your bees using dressmaker's carbon paper – white is best on darker fabrics.

3. Add a sheet of backing and use a large embroidery hoop so the hoop is filled with one of the bees.

4. Start with the body of the bee. Thread the needle with six strands of white embroidery thread and begin to split stitch the bee's body. You don't have to be too neat with this as I think this adds to the textured look of the body.

5. Re-thread the needle with two strands of white embroidery thread – this will make the legs appear more detailed and dainty compared to the body.

6. Back stitch the legs, following the carbon lines – try to keep the stitches equal.

7. Add a simple running stitch for the antennae – again, so these appear more delicate.

1. You could go all out with this design
    and add a colourful flower between the bees.
2. Adding a layer of appliqué black lace on the body
    of the bee is an alternative to the beading, which
    would add some lovely texture and subtle pattern.

8. Thread the needle with metallic gold thread. (This can be a little tricky as metallic thread tends to fray really easily, so I add a little tape to the end of the thread to make it easier to thread through the needle. Just remove the tape once threaded.)

9. Using a wider back stitch, work around the wings with the metallic thread, using shorter lengths of metallic thread so it's easier to work with, avoiding breakages.

10. Fill areas of the body with beads! I opted for gold beads which I randomly stitched within a section of the bee's body to create a 3D look. Adding beads looks tricky but it's not, it's just a case of adding a knot to the back of the fabric, coming up through to the front and attaching the bead, then stitching another knot to secure.

11. Repeat the steps for the other bee. I decided not to add beads to this one so there was a contrast, but add as little or as much embellishment as you wish.

Acknowledgements

Thank you to everyone at Kyle Books, especially Isabel for giving me the opportunity to create this book. Thanks also to Kim Lightbody and Evi and Susan at Evi-O.Studio for bringing my vision to life so perfectly.

To my parents Mark and Kay, for teaching me to believe I can achieve anything I put my mind to and encouraging my creativity endlessly. Even if that does mean putting up with the trail of threads, beads and sequins I leave wherever I go! Thank you for being the best parents I could have ever wished for. Love you lots!

To Kirsty, thank you for being the best sister and friend I could ask for. For your pep talks and positivity and for being the rock of the family that everyone can depend on.

To George, for pretending to love all the visits to craft shops, for being my number one fan, believing in me and putting up with my midnight worries. You are forever telling me how proud you are of me but I couldn't do any of it without you.

To Nanny Warren, who encouraged me to keep everything and make pretty things out of them.

To Steph, for being my partner in crime, getting me through university with our constant singing duets! You are a true best friend.

To Jayne, for being like a second mum to me and for being my dearest friend.

To my Dobermann puppy, Bea, for providing endless cuddles.

To my entire family, I am lucky to have you all.

Thank you to everyone who has ever purchased anything from me, bought this book or followed my business journey, you have allowed me to work on something I love and have my dream job.

. . . .

Resources

Hobbycraft
www.hobbycraft.co.uk

John Lewis
www.johnlewis.com

Joann
www.joann.com

Fabric Land
www.fabricland.co.uk

Sew and So
www.sewandso.co.uk

Etsy
www.etsy.com

Ebay
www.ebay.com

Amazon
www.Amazon.com

Josy Rose
(Best for sequins/beads)
www.josyrose.com